GREENTOWN SCHOOL

SPINOSAURUS

THE THORN LIZARD

BY DAVID WEST

PowerKiDS
press

New York

Published in 2012 by The Rosen Publishing Group, Inc.
29 East 21st Street, New York 10010

Designed and produced by
David West Books

Designed and written by David West

Photographic credits: 30, Kabacchi

Library of Congress Cataloging-in-Publication Data
West, David (David William), 1956–
Spinosaurus : the thorn lizard / By David West.
    pages cm. — (Graphic Dinosaurs)
    Includes index.
ISBN 978-1-4488-5203-1 (library binding) — ISBN 978-1-4488-5244-4 (pbk.)
    — ISBN 978-1-4488-5245-1 (6-pack)
    1. Spinosaurus—Juvenile literature. I. Title.
QE862.S3W467 2012
    567.912—dc22

2010048992

Manufactured in China

CPSIA Compliance Information: Batch #DS1102PK:
For Further Information contact Rosen Publishing, New York,
New York at 1-800-237-9932

CONTENTS

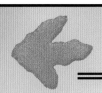

WHAT IS A SPINOSAURUS?

SPINOSAURUS MEANS "THORN LIZARD."

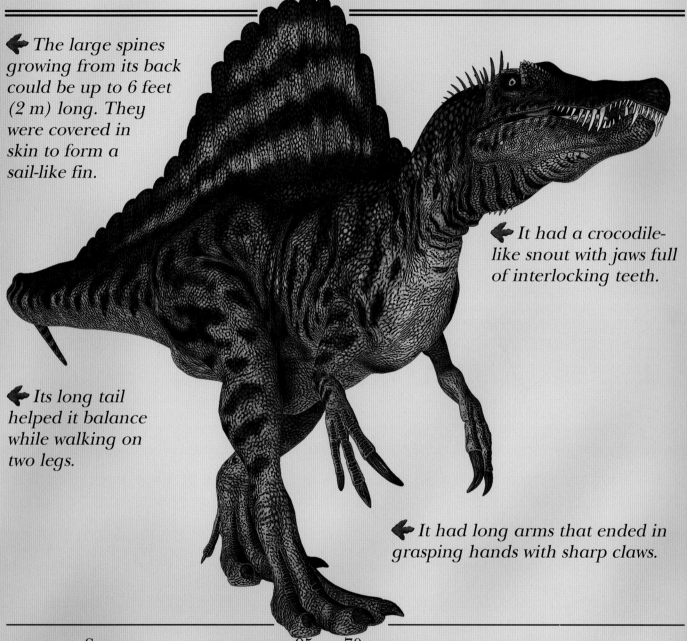

◀ The large spines growing from its back could be up to 6 feet (2 m) long. They were covered in skin to form a sail-like fin.

◀ It had a crocodile-like snout with jaws full of interlocking teeth.

◀ Its long tail helped it balance while walking on two legs.

◀ It had long arms that ended in grasping hands with sharp claws.

SPINOSAURUS LIVED AROUND 95 TO 70 MILLION YEARS AGO, DURING THE **CRETACEOUS PERIOD. FOSSILS** OF ITS SKELETON HAVE BEEN FOUND IN NORTH AFRICA (SEE PAGE 30).

◀ Adult Spinosauruses measured up to 59 feet (18 m) long and weighed about 8 tons (7 t).

SAIL-LIKE FIN

The fin on Spinosaurus's back probably had lots of blood vessels. This would have helped control its temperature. The sail acted like a car's radiator, helping cool the blood in a breeze (just as modern elephants use their ears to keep cool). It may also have helped warm up the dinosaur when the Sun's rays hit it on cooler mornings.

An African elephant uses its ears to keep cool.

Grizzly bears eat fish, meat, and berries.

CROCODILE-LIKE SNOUT

Spinosauruses' jaws were similar to those of a crocodile. **Paleontologists** think that, like a crocodile, it fed on fish and other animals that lived in or near the water. It is also likely that it **preyed** on dinosaurs.

A modern crocodile

LIFESTYLE

Fossil evidence suggests that it walked on two legs and spent some time in the water. Spinosaurus was an **opportunist**—this makes it the Cretaceous equivalent of a large grizzly bear. It mostly fished, but it also **scavenged**, eating many different kinds of small and medium prey.

PART ONE

BREAKFAST

IT IS EARLY MORNING IN NORTH AFRICA DURING THE LATE CRETACEOUS PERIOD. THE SUN'S RAYS BREAK THROUGH THE FOREST CANOPY, WARMING THE SAIL OF A SLEEPING SPINOSAURUS. IT IS A LARGE MALE WEIGHING ALMOST 8 TONS (7 T).

MOSQUITOES DANCE AROUND ITS HEAD. THEY BOTHER THE SPINOSAURUS AS THEY GET IN ITS EYES AND NOSTRILS.

THE SPINOSAURUS IS HUNGRY AND THIRSTY. IT RAISES ITS MASSIVE BODY AND HEADS OFF TOWARD A NEARBY RIVER.

SUDDENLY, IT HEARS AND SMELLS FRESH KILL BEING EATEN. IT MOVES FORWARD CAREFULLY.

SNIFF

IN A CLEARING IS A GROUP OF CARCHARODONTOSAURUSES THAT ARE FEEDING ON A YOUNG AEGYPTOSAURUS THEY HAVE JUST KILLED.

NORMALLY THE SPINOSAURUS WOULD CHARGE IN AND USE ITS SIZE TO SCARE THE **PREDATORS** AWAY FROM THEIR MEAL. BUT IN THIS CASE THERE ARE TOO MANY OF THESE GIANT CARNIVORES, WHICH CAN BE UP TO 50 FEET (15 M) LONG. IT SLINKS AWAY WITHOUT BEING NOTICED BY THEM.

THE SPINOSAURUS FINALLY ARRIVES AT THE RIVER AND DRINKS FROM THE FRESH, RUNNING WATER.

SLURRP

THE SPINOSAURUS IS NOT FAR FROM THE COAST. IT WALKS ALONG THE RIVERBANK TOWARD THE SEA, WHERE IT KNOWS THERE IS GOOD HUNTING AND FISHING. A LONE COLOBORHYNCHUS GLIDES ABOVE IT, HEADED IN THE SAME DIRECTION.

WHERE IT ARRIVES AT THE COAST, THE RIVER BREAKS UP INTO MANY CHANNELS. IT IS A DELTA, AND TO EITHER SIDE, WHERE THE SALTY WATER MEETS THE LAND, MANGROVE TREES GROW.

THE SPINOSAURUS ENTERS THE MANGROVES AND SLOWLY MOVES ALONG THE CHANNELS BETWEEN THE TREES.

AS ITS SHADOW PASSES OVER THE YOUNG PLESIOSAURS AND FISH, THEY SCATTER INTO THE SAFETY OF THE MANGROVE ROOTS.

IT FREEZES AS IT SPOTS A SMALL SHARK SWIMMING TOWARD IT.

IN AN INSTANT THE SPINOSAURUS SNAPS UP THE SHARK WITH ITS CROCODILE-LIKE JAWS. IT MAKES A TASTY BREAKFAST SNACK.

THERE IS NO BREEZE IN THE MANGROVES, AND THE SPINOSAURUS IS BEGINNING TO OVERHEAT. THE MOSQUITOES ARE ALSO BEGINNING TO BOTHER IT AGAIN. IT MOVES OUT ONTO THE SANDY CORAL FLATS, WHERE THE SEA BREEZE COOLS THE BLOOD PASSING THROUGH ITS SAIL.

OUT ON A SANDBAR IT SEES A **PTEROSAUR** PECKING AT THE REMAINS OF A TURTLE SHELL. IT IS AN ALANQA. IT HASN'T SEEN IT, SO IT APPROACHES SLOWLY.

SUDDENLY A DELTADROMEUS DARTS OUT FROM A PATCH OF MANGROVES AND HEADS FOR THE ALANQA.

THE ALANQA SEES THE DELTADROMEUS AND TAKES TO THE AIR JUST IN TIME.

IT FLIES LOW OVER THE WAVES.

SUDDENLY A GIANT TYLOSAURUS LEAPS FROM THE OCEAN AND GRASPS THE PTEROSAUR IN ITS JAWS.

SPLOOSH

THE DELTADROMEUS IS TOO SPEEDY FOR THE SPINOSAURUS TO CATCH AND DISAPPEARS INTO THE MANGROVES. THE SPINOSAURUS HEADS OFF ALONG THE COAST IN SEARCH OF LUNCH.

PART TWO

A LIGHT LUNCH

IT IS MIDDAY AND IT IS VERY HOT. THE SPINOSAURUS IS HOT AND HUNGRY. IT HAS BEEN WALKING ALONG ITS HUNTING GROUND ON THE COAST OF NORTH AFRICA, AND IT HAS NOT EATEN ANYTHING SINCE BREAKFAST.

IT SPOTS ANOTHER SPINOSAURUS. IT IS A JUVENILE AND IT HAS INVADED THE SPINOSAURUS'S TERRITORY.

THE SPINOSAURUS CHASES AFTER IT.

ROAAAAAR

THE JUVENILE RUNS INTO THE SEA AND BEGINS SWIMMING ACROSS A LARGE CHANNEL OF DEEP WATER.

GRAAAARRR

THE JUVENILE IS A FASTER SWIMMER AND BEGINS TO PULL AWAY FROM THE OLDER SPINOSAURUS.

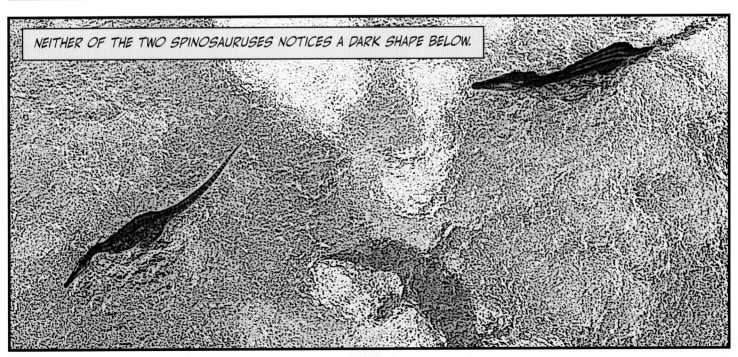

NEITHER OF THE TWO SPINOSAURUSES NOTICES A DARK SHAPE BELOW.

IT IS THE TYLOSAURUS, AND IT LAUNCHES ITS ATTACK FROM BELOW. IT CATCHES THE JUVENILE IN ITS MOUTH.

AS IT DRAGS THE STRUGGLING JUVENILE UNDER THE WAVES, THE SPINOSAURUS HEADS BACK TO SHORE.

KERSPLOOSH

THE SPINOSAURUS MOVES ALONG THE COAST TO AN AREA OF CORAL FLATS. THE TIDE IS GOING OUT AND IT KNOWS LARGE FISH WILL BE SWIMMING THROUGH THE CHANNELS. IT SEES SIGNS THAT THERE ARE FISH AROUND. COLOBORHYNCHUSES ARE FEEDING ON SCHOOLS OF SMALLER FISH.

IT IS ABOUT TO STEP INTO THE WATER WHEN A LARGE SHAPE SWIMS BY. IT'S A STOMATOSUCHUS, A LARGE, 30-FOOT (9 M) LONG, CROCODILE-LIKE REPTILE.

IT HAS A LARGE POUCH LIKE A PELICAN'S AND FEEDS ON FISH. THE SPINOSAURUS STAYS AWAY.

THE SPINOSAURUS WALKS FARTHER ALONG THE COAST AND FINDS A SPOT THAT LOOKS GOOD FOR FISHING. A LONE ALANQA PERCHES ON A MANGROVE.

THE SPINOSAURUS POSITIONS ITSELF AT THE EDGE OF A SMALL CHANNEL BEHIND A CORAL OUTCROP. THE TIDE IS RUSHING OUT AND THE BIG FISH ARE LEAVING THE SHALLOWS. THEY HEAD FOR DEEPER WATER ALONG THE CHANNELS.

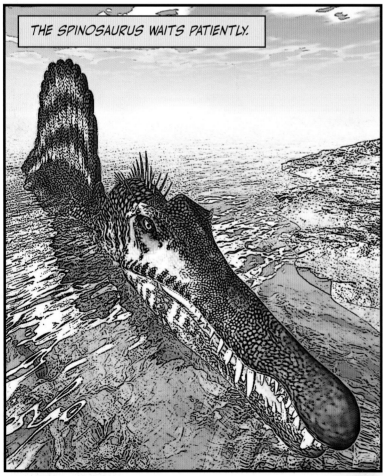

THE SPINOSAURUS WAITS PATIENTLY.

SOON A LARGE FISH HEADS DOWN THE CHANNEL.

IT LUNGES AT IT AND GRASPS THE FISH WITH ITS SHARP TEETH.

SPLOSH

IT CARRIES THE FISH FLAPPING TO THE SHALLOWS AND CONSUMES IT IN A COUPLE OF SWALLOWS.

THE SPINOSAURUS RETURNS TO ITS SPOT BUT IT IS OUT OF LUCK. AFTER WAITING FOR AN HOUR WITHOUT SUCCESS, IT GIVES UP. THE BREEZE HAS LET UP AND IT IS FEELING THE HEAT AGAIN.

IT HEADS OFF TO A SHADED CREEK.

PART THREE... NO SNACKS

AS IT WALKS UP THE CREEK THE SPINOSAURUS PASSES A GIANT TITANOSAUR FEEDING ON THE HIGH BRANCHES OF A TREE. IT'S A PARALITITAN. AT 65 TONS AND OVER 90 FEET LONG IT IS TOO BIG EVEN FOR SPINOSAURUS TO TAKE ON.

THE PARALITITAN CONTINUES FEEDING AS THE SPINOSAURUS KEEPS WALKING UPSTREAM.

AS IT WALKS AROUND A BEND IN THE CREEK, THE SPINOSAURUS DISTURBS A COUPLE OF RUGOPSES. THEY HAVE BEEN FEEDING ON EGGS FROM A TURTLE'S NEST.

CRUNCH

BEFORE THE SPINOSAURUS HAS A CHANCE TO REACT THE TWO RUGOPS RUN OFF INTO THE UNDERGROWTH.

THE CREEK SUDDENLY OPENS UP INTO A LARGE LAKE. IT IS A LAGOON, A SHALLOW AREA OF SEAWATER THAT HAS BEEN CUT OFF FROM THE SEA BY A THIN CREST OF LAND.

THE SPINOSAURUS WADES INTO THE LAGOON. SCHOOLS OF SMALL FISH SCATTER IN FRONT OF IT.

IN THE DEEPER PARTS THE SPINOSAURUS SWIMS UNDER THE SURFACE, LOOKING FOR SOMETHING TO EAT. A SMALL CROCODILIAN HIDES UNDER AN OLD TREE TRUNK.

ON THE OPPOSITE BANK, A GIANT 40-FOOT (12 M) LONG SARCOSUCHUS HAS BEEN WATCHING THE SPINOSAURUS.

IT SLIPS INTO THE WATER.

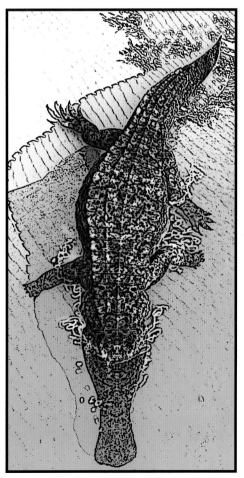

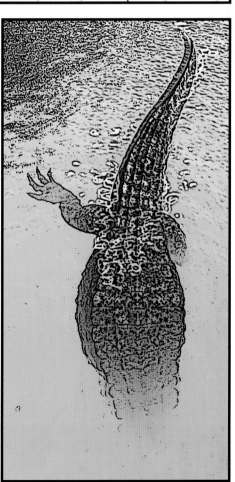

THE SPINOSAURUS HAS REACHED A SHALLOW PART OF THE LAGOON. IT IS STALKING A LARGE FISH FEEDING AMONG SOME DEAD MANGROVES.

IT DOES NOT NOTICE WHAT LOOKS LIKE A LARGE LOG MOVING SLOWLY TOWARD IT.

IT IS THE SARCOSUCHUS. IT LAUNCHES ITSELF AT THE UNSUSPECTING SPINOSAURUS.

SPLOOSH

THE SPINOSAURUS ACTS SWIFTLY AND TWISTS TO DODGE THE GIANT JAWS OF THE SARCOSUCHUS.

GRAAARRGH

THE SPINOSAURUS REALIZES THAT THE SARCOSUCHUS IS TOO HEAVILY ARMORED FOR ITS TEETH TO PIERCE THE SKIN. SO IT RUNS TO THE SAFETY OF THE SHORELINE.

THE SPINOSAURUS HAS HAD A LUCKY ESCAPE. A FRESH BREEZE BRINGS THE SMELL OF A RECENT KILL, AND IT HEADS OFF TO FIND THE SOURCE.

PART FOUR

DINNER IS SERVED

AARRK

AARRK

AARRK

AARRK

ITS JOURNEY TAKES IT BACK TO THE COAST. IT IS LATE
AFTERNOON AND THE SPINOSAURUS IS VERY HUNGRY. IN THE
SHALLOWS LIES A PLESIOSAUR. IT IS A THILILUA, AND IT HAS
BEACHED ITSELF AFTER BEING ATTACKED BY THE TYLOSAURUS.
THE SPINOSAURUS CAN SEE ALANQAS FEEDING FROM ITS BACK.

A DELTADROMEUS RACES ACROSS THE SAND.

A COLOBORHYNCHUS ATTEMPTS TO TAKE OFF, BUT IT IS TOO SLOW.

GRAARRK

THREE BAHARIASAURUSES APPEAR AND HEAD STRAIGHT FOR THE THILILUA.

AARRK

AARRK

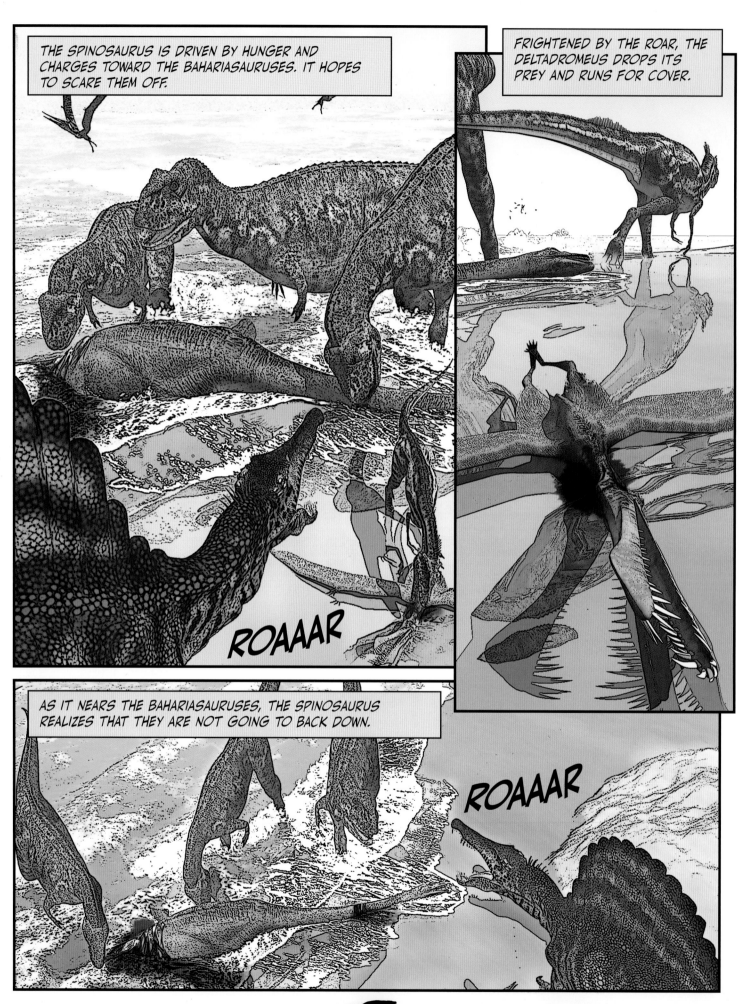

THE SPINOSAURUS IS DRIVEN BY HUNGER AND CHARGES TOWARD THE BAHARIASAURUSES. IT HOPES TO SCARE THEM OFF.

FRIGHTENED BY THE ROAR, THE DELTADROMEUS DROPS ITS PREY AND RUNS FOR COVER.

ROAAAR

AS IT NEARS THE BAHARIASAURUSES, THE SPINOSAURUS REALIZES THAT THEY ARE NOT GOING TO BACK DOWN.

ROAAAR

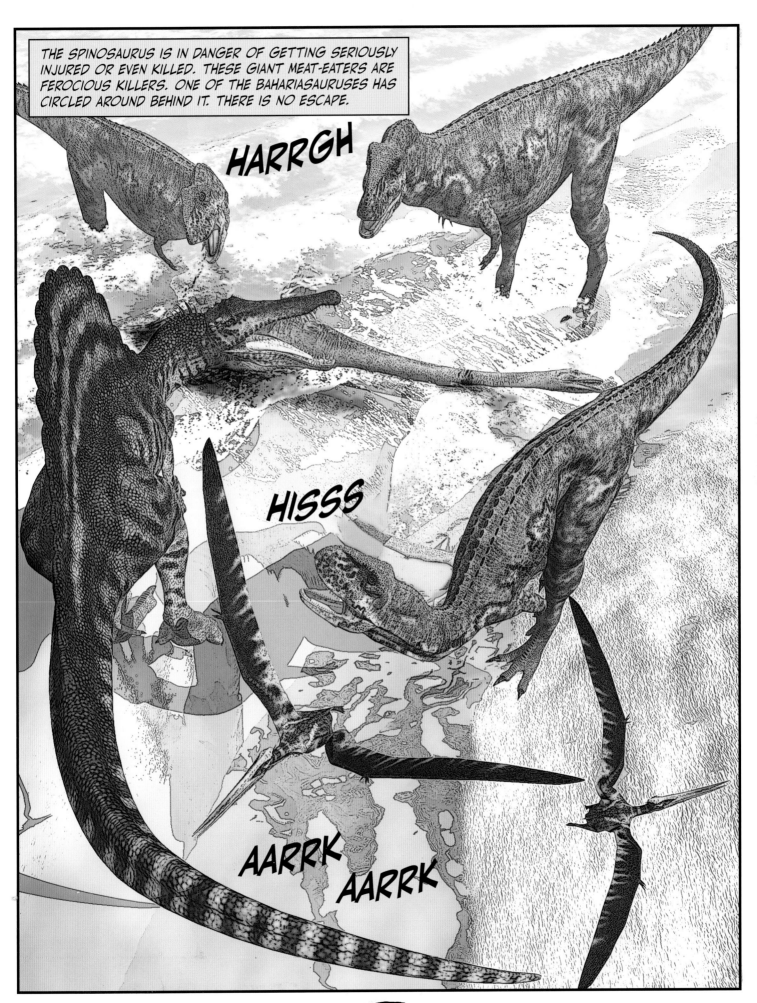

THE SPINOSAURUS IS IN DANGER OF GETTING SERIOUSLY INJURED OR EVEN KILLED. THESE GIANT MEAT-EATERS ARE FEROCIOUS KILLERS. ONE OF THE BAHARIASAURUSES HAS CIRCLED AROUND BEHIND IT. THERE IS NO ESCAPE.

HARRGH

HISSS

AARRK AARRK

SUDDENLY THE WATER ERUPTS. THE TYLOSAURUS HAS SWUM UP A DEEP CHANNEL AFTER THE THILILUA. IT HAS SEEN ONE OF THE BAHARIASAURUSES AND GRASPS IT BY ITS LEG.

WAAARGH

KERSPLOOSH

AS THE SECOND BAHARIASAURUS TURNS TO SEE WHAT THE NOISE IS, THE SPINOSAURUS ATTACKS. IT GRASPS THE BAHARIASAURUS BY THE HEAD, AND ITS POWERFUL JAWS BREAK ITS NECK.

THE THIRD BAHARIASAURUS, FACED WITH THE SNARLING SPINOSAURUS, RUNS FOR ITS LIFE.

GNAAARGH

THE SPINOSAURUS DRAGS THE THILILUA UP THE BEACH. IT THEN BEGINS TO FEED. FINALLY, IN THE LATE EVENING, IT HAS A MEAL TO SATISFY ITS HUNGER.

FOSSIL EVIDENCE

WE CAN GET A GOOD IDEA OF WHAT DINOSAURS MAY HAVE LOOKED LIKE FROM THEIR FOSSILS. FOSSILS ARE FORMED WHEN THE HARD PARTS OF AN ANIMAL OR PLANT ARE BURIED AND THEN TURN TO ROCK OVER MILLIONS OF YEARS.

Although it is the largest meat-eating dinosaur discovered so far, very little fossil evidence of Spinosaurus has been found. Fossils discovered in the 1910s were destroyed during World War II (although detailed drawings and descriptions of the fossils survived). Since then fossils of parts of Spinosaurus's skull have been discovered. Paleontologists have been able to build up an idea of what Spinosaurus may have looked like and how it lived from fossil finds of other spinosaurids such as Baryonyx and Irritator. Scientists have discovered fossilized fish scales and bones from a young Iguanodon in the rib cage of Baryonyx fossils. A spinosaur tooth stuck in a South American pterosaur bone suggests that spinosaurs occasionally preyed on these flying reptiles.

A reconstruction of a Spinosaurus skeleton

ANIMAL GALLERY

ALL THESE ANIMALS APPEAR IN THE STORY.

Alanqa
Arabic for "phoenix"
Wingspan: 13 ft (4 m)
A large flying reptile

Coloborhynchus
"Maimed beak"
Wingspan: 20 ft (6 m)
A giant flying reptile

Thililua
Named after an ancient
Berber god
Length: 20 ft (6 m)
A long-necked marine
reptile

Rugops
"Wrinkle face"
Length: 23 ft (7 m)
A medium-sized
meat-eating scavenger

Deltadromeus
"Delta runner"
Length: 26.5 ft (8 m)
A swift, slender,
meat-eating dinosaur

Stomatosuchus
"Mouth crocodile"
Length: 33 ft (10 m)
A large distant relative of
crocodiles, with a pelicanlike
pouch

Bahariasaurus
"Bahariya lizard"
Length: 39 ft (12 m)
A large meat-eating dinosaur

Sarcosuchus
"Flesh crocodile"
Length: 40 ft (12.2 m)
A giant distant relative
of crocodiles

Tylosaurus
"Knob lizard"
Length: 49 ft (15 m)
A large predatory marine
lizard

Carcharodontosaurus
"Carcharodon lizard"
Length: 49 ft (15 m)
A huge, meat-eating dinosaur

Aegyptosaurus
"Egyptian lizard"
Length: 49 ft (15 m)
A long-necked dinosaur

Paralititan
"Tidal giant"
Length: 92 ft (28 m)
A giant long-necked dinosaur

GLOSSARY

Cretaceous period (krih-TAY-shus PIR-ee-ud) The period of time between 145 million and 65 million years ago.

fossils (FO-sulz) The remains of living things that have turned to rock.

opportunist (o-per-TOO-nist) An animal that will adapt and take advantage of any new situation.

paleontologists (pay-lee-on-TAH-luh-jists) Scientists who study fossils.

predators (PREH-duh-terz) Animals that hunt animals.

preyed (PRAYD) Hunted for smaller animals.

pterosaur (TER-uh-sawr) A flying reptile that was around during the time of the dinosaurs.

scavenged (SKA-venjd) Searched for and fed on animals that are already dead.

INDEX

Web Sites
Due to the changing nature of Internet links, The Rosen Publishing Group, Inc., has developed an online list of Web sites related to the subject of this book. This site is updated regularly. Please use this link to access the list:
www.powerkidslinks.com/gdino/spino/